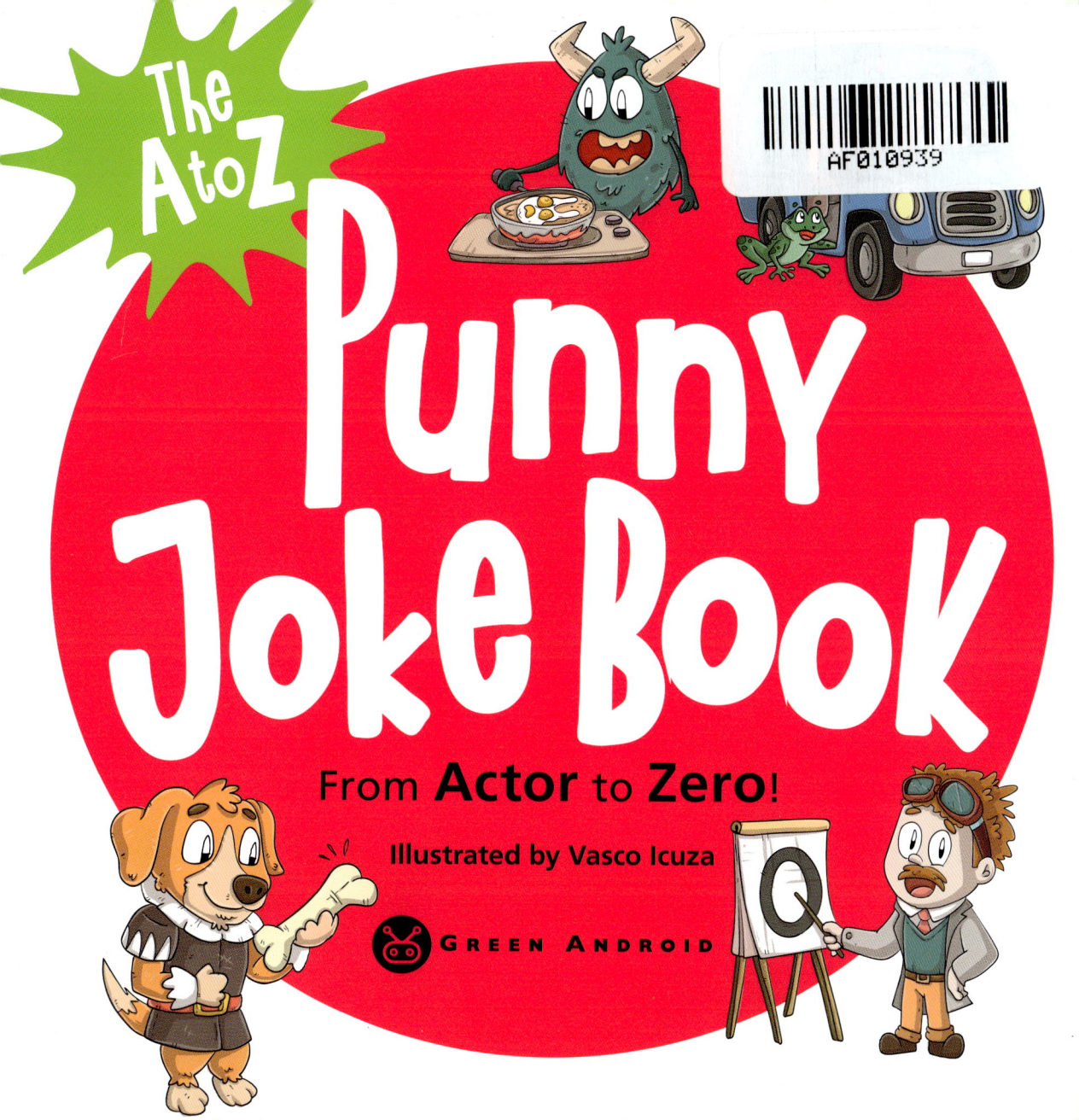

The A to Z Punny Joke Book

If you love great puns that make you chuckle, laugh and groan, then this is the book for you!

The A to Z Punny Joke Book is a grin-inducing collection of over 300 hilarious one-liners. The jokes are ordered alphabetically, so you can chuckle your way from A to Z, or search for a joke about your favourite subject. From absurd actors to zany zeroes, the laughs don't stop!

The A to Z Punny Joke Book is all you need to have a *pun-derful* joke-telling time!

Q Did you hear about the glassblower who **ACCIDENTALLY** inhaled?
A He got a stomach pane!

Q Why should you say "break a leg" to an **ACTOR**?
A Because every play needs a cast!

Q Why do dogs make such good **ACTORS**?
A They know how to paws for dramatic effect!

Q What is the definition of **ACUPUNCTURE**?
A A jab well done!

Q Did you hear about the man that sued an **AIRLINE** company after it lost his luggage?
A Sadly, he lost his case!

Q What does **ALGAE** do when it's in trouble?
A Sea kelp!

Q What do you call a thieving **ALLIGATOR**?
A A crook-odile!

Q What kind of dog is always **AMAZED**?
A A chi-wow-ah!

Q What two people always travel in an **AMBULANCE**?
A A pair-a-medics!

Q What's it like to eavesdrop on two croaking **AMPHIBIANS**?
A It's toad-ally ribbet-ing!

Q What happened when the **AQUATIC** mammals escaped from the zoo?
A It was otter chaos!

Q Why should you never argue with an **ARCHAEOLOGIST**?
A They always dig up the past!

Q Why can't you rearrange a meeting with an **ARCHITECT**?
A Because they make concrete plans!

Q What should you do if you can't spell **ARMAGEDDON**?
A Don't worry, it's not the end of the world!

Q What is always on its way but never **ARRIVES**?
A Tomorrow!

Q Why did the **BANK** manager leave his job?
A He lost interest in it!

Q Did you know that **BIGFOOT** is often confused with Sasquatch?
A Yeti never complains!

Q Did you know that it's impossible for one **BIRD** to make a pun?
A But toucan!

Q What part of the **BODY** always loses?
A De-feat!

Q Why should you consider eating a hard-**BOILED** egg for breakfast?
A It's hard to beat!

Q Did you hear about the child who spent all day reading **BOOKS**?
A It was bound to happen!

Q What should you do if you forget how to use a **BOOMERANG**?
A Just wait, it'll eventually come back to you!

Q What should you do if your **BOYFRIEND** doesn't appreciate fresh fruit?
A Let that mango!

Q What did the **BUS** driver say to the frog?
A "Hop on!"

Q What do **BUTTERFLIES** sleep on?
A Cater-pillows!

Q What type of **CAN** doesn't need a can opener?
A A pelican!

Q Which country's **CAPITAL** has the fastest-growing population?
A Ireland. Every day it's Dublin!

Q What do you call an animal you keep in your **CAR**?
A A carpet!

Q Why isn't my **CAT** a good storyteller?
A Because it only has one tale!

Q Why aren't **CATS** funny?
A Their jokes are a-paw-ling!

Q What did the **CEDAR** tree say to the maple tree?

A "What's sap?"

Q Why did the cat eat some **CHEESE**?

A So, it could wait for the mouse with baited breath!

Q Why is it hard to make a new **CHEMISTRY** joke?

A All the good ones argon!

Q How much does a **CHIMNEY** cost?

A Nothing, it's on the house!

Q What's the best time on a **CLOCK**?

A 6:30, hands down!

Q What should you tell your friend when they say they don't understand **CLONING**?
A "That makes two of us!"

Q What do you call it when a **CLOWN** holds the door open for you?
A A nice jester!

Q What type of **COAT** is wet?
A A coat of paint!

Q Why does **COFFEE** hate mornings?
A It keeps getting mugged!

Q What do you eat when you're **COLD** and angry?
A A brr-grr!

Q What is a cat's favourite **COLOUR**?
A Purrr-ple!

Q Why should you never **COMBINE** a cat with an apostrophe?
A It's sure to be a catastrophe!

Q Which bear is the most **CONDESCENDING**?
A A pan-duh!

Q What part of a house are dogs best at **CONSTRUCTING**?
A The roof!

Q Did you hear about the **CONSTRUCTION** workers who can cut a piece of wood by looking at it?
A It's true, they saw it with their own eyes!

Q What's the corniest part of a **CORN** field?
A The corner!

Q What should a lawyer always wear to **COURT**?
A A good lawsuit!

Q Why do **COWS** produce more milk when a farmer talks to them?
A It's a case of in one ear and out the udder!

Q Did you hear about the ice-cream van that **CRASHED**?
A The driver blamed it on the rocky road!

Q Why is it so hard to make plans with a **CROISSANT**?
A It's so flaky!

Q What's the best thing about telling **DAD** jokes?
A He sometimes laughs!

Q What do you do if your friend **DAVID** has his ID stolen?
A Call him Dav from now on!

Q How far is it to the **DENTIST'S** office?
A Six smiles!

Q Who is the most famous scarecrow **DETECTIVE**?
A Strawlock Holmes!

Q What's the only word that's spelled incorrectly in the **DICTIONARY**?
A Incorrectly!

Q Why did the house go to the **DOCTOR**?
A It had a windowpane!

Q What do you call a **DOG** that practises magic?
A A Labra-cadabra-dor!

Q When is a door not a **DOOR**?
A When it's ajar!

Q What do you call it when you **DREAM** in colour?
A A pigment of your imagination!

Q What did the **DRUMMER** name her twin daughters?
A Anna 1, Anna 2!

Q What kind of car does an **EGG** drive?
A A yolks-wagen!

Q Who solves mysteries involving **ELECTRICITY**?
A Sherlock Ohms!

Q Why is dark spelled with a k and not a c at the **END**?
A Because you cannot c in the dark!

Q Why are **ENGLISH** teachers the best?
A They never write their students off!

Q What is life like for an **ESCALATOR** repairman?
A It has its ups and downs!

Q What should you do if you're terrified of **ESCALATORS**?
A Take steps to avoid them!

Q What did the **EVIL** chicken lay?
A Devilled eggs!

Q Did you hear about the vegetable **EXPLORER**?
A It went off to discover un-chard-ed territories!

Q Where do **EXTINCT** animals go to eat?
A The diner-soar!

HAW-HAW!

Q If jokes about feet are corny, what are jokes about **EYES**?
A Cornea!

Q Did you hear about the worker that lost his job at the calendar **FACTORY**?

A He got fired for taking a few days off!

Q Why do judges make good tooth **FAIRIES**?

A Because they want the tooth, the whole tooth and nothing but the tooth!

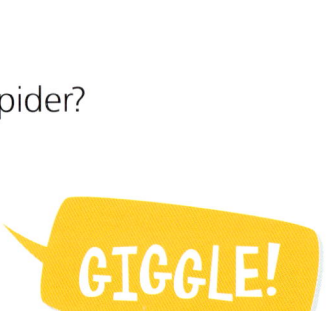

Q Why are some **FAIRY** tales too long?

A They have a tendency to dragon!

Q What did the **FATHER** spider say to the child spider?

A "You're spending too much time on the web!"

Q What's a farmer's **FAVOURITE** mythical animal?

A The unicorn!

GIGGLE!

Q What do you call a **FEAR** of giants?
A A fee-fi-phobia!

Q Ever wondered how I **FEEL** about cat puns?
A "They freak meow-t! Seriously, I'm not kitten!"

Q What's a **FELINE'S** favourite novel?
A The Great Catsby!

Q How do **FESTIVE** dogs greet each other?
A Happy howl-idays!

Q How did the two cats end their **FIGHT**?
A They hissed and made up!

Q Why are your **FINGERS** the most reliable part of your body?
A You can always count on them!

Q Why did the man lie down in the **FIREPLACE**?
A He wanted to sleep like a log!

Q Why is it so hard to get a **FISH** to talk about its feelings?
A Because it's being a little koi!

Q How much are **FLAT** batteries?
A They are free of charge!

Q What did the big flower say to the little **FLOWER**?
A "Hey, Bud!"

Q Why is Peter Pan always **FLYING**?
A He Never-lands!

Q What's a **FORKLIFT**?
A Food, usually!

Q Where do cows go for **FUN**?
A To the a-moos-ment park!

Q How much room should you give **FUNGI** to grow?
A As mushroom as possible!

Q What happens if you boil a **FUNNY** bone?
A You make a laughing stock!

Q How do you know if a **GARDENER** is not good at her job?
A Her work is a little rough around the hedges!

Q Do **GERMAN** cats have multiple lives?
A Nein!

Q Why do **GHOSTS** like to ride in lifts?
A It elevates their spirits!

Q When is the best time to open a **GIFT**?
A The present!

Q How would you feel if both your **GLOVES** were for left hands?
A On the one hand it would be great, but on the other it wouldn't be right!

Q Why didn't the children tell their mother that they ate some **GLUE**?

A Their lips were sealed!

Q How does a lawyer say **GOODBYE**?

A "I'll be suing ya!"

Q What's a **GRANDMA'S** favourite fruit?

A Elderberry!

Q Why should you tell everyone about the benefits of eating dried **GRAPES**?

A It's all about raisin awareness!

Q Why should you be suspicious of someone carrying **GRAPH** paper?

A They might be plotting something!

CACKLE!

Q What did one blade of **GRASS** say to another about the lack of rain?
A "I guess we'll just have to make dew!"

Q Why would a **GRIZZLY** hate this book?
A They can't bear puns!

Q What does a little pun become when it **GROWS** older?
A Fully groan!

Q Why did the **GYM** close down?
A It just didn't work out!

Q How long does it take for a **GYMNAST** to get to practice?
A A split second!

Q Why did the carrot make a **HAIR** appointment?
A Its roots were showing!

Q What type of person goes to the ice rink when it's **HALF** price?
A A cheapskate!

Q What happened to the **HAMBURGER** that missed too much school?
A It had to stay after school to ketchup!

Q Did you hear about the **HARDWORKING** lettuce?
A It was promoted to head of its department!

Q Did you hear about the guy stuck in a **HEAVY** metal box?
A Don't worry, he's safe now!

Q Why should you never give a gift to a **HISTORY** teacher?
A They don't like the present!

Q What do bees do after they build a new **HIVE**?
A They throw a house-swarming party!

Q What can you **HOLD** without touching it?
A A conversation!

Q What kind of keys do **HOMEMADE** gingerbread men carry?
A Cook-keys!

Q Did you hear about the man in the hospital with a plastic **HORSE** in his stomach?
A His condition is stable!

Q Why are **HOUSES** with basements popular?
A Because they are best-cellars!

Q How do you know that cats have a great sense of **HUMOUR**?
A They're a-mew-sed by hiss-terical jokes!

Q Have you heard the sad news of **HUMPTY DUMPTY**?
A His life is in pieces and he feels like one big yoke!

Q Did you hear about the **HUNGRY** clock?
A It went back four seconds!

Q Did you hear about the athlete who was scared of **HURDLES**?
A She got over it eventually!

Q Why do **ICE-CREAM** cones carry umbrellas?

A Because there's always a chance of sprinkles!

Q Why is it a bad **IDEA** to eat a clock?

A It's so time-consuming!

Q Why should you never discuss **INFINITY** with mathematicians?

A They can go on about it forever!

Q How does a pizza **INTRODUCE** itself?

A "Slice to meet you!"

Q How do you keep **INTRUDERS** out of a castle made of cheese?

A Build a moat-zarella!

Q Why did the painting go to **JAIL**?
A It was framed!

Q What would happen if you accidentally drank a **JAR** of invisible ink?
A You'd have to go to the hospital and wait to be seen!

Q Did you hear the **JOKE** about the TV controller?
A It wasn't remotely funny!

Q Why am I the champ of telling punny **JOKES**?
A "It's just how eye roll!"

Q What did the **JUDGE** name her daughter?
A Sue!

Q What do you call a lazy **KANGAROO**?
A A pouch potato!

Q Why should you never trust car **KEYS**?
A They're always starting something!

Q Why did the kid get **KICKED** out of the secret cooking society?
A He spilled the beans!

Q Did you hear about the **KID** who fainted at school?
A She went down in history!

Q Did you hear that there was a **KIDNAPPING** at school yesterday?
A Don't worry, she woke up!

Q What would happen if we changed from **KILOGRAMS** to pounds?
A There would be mass confusion!

Q Why should you always be **KIND** to dentists?
A They have fillings too!

Q Why was **KING** Arthur's army too tired to fight?
A It had a lot of sleepless knights!

Q Why can't you explain puns to **KLEPTOMANIACS**?
A They always take things literally!

Q What do you call a **KNIGHT** who is afraid to fight?
A Sir Render!

Q What do you call a **LAMB** that is always quiet?
A A shhhheep!

Q Did you hear about the chicken-proof front **LAWN**?
A It's impeccable!

Q What kind of exercises do **LAZY** people do?
A Diddly-squats!

Q What did the **LEG** say to the foot?
A "It's going tibia k!"

Q What do you call the **LETTUCE** left over after you make a salad?
A The romaine-der!

Q What did the **LIBRARIAN** say when the books were a mess?

A "We ought to be ashamed of our shelves!"

Q Why couldn't the couple get married at the **LIBRARY**?

A It was fully booked!

Q What has more **LIVES** than a cat?

A A frog! It croaks every day!

Q What do you call a **LOBSTER** that's afraid of tight spaces?

A Claw-strophobic!

Q Why did the man learn to pick **LOCKS**?

A He thought it would open a lot of doors for him!

Q What type of dog can work as a **LOCKSMITH**?

A A corg-key!

Q What do you call a magician that **LOSES** his magic?

A Ian!

CHUCKLE!

Q What's the difference between a security password and glass **LUGGAGE**?

A One's case sensitive and the other's a sensitive case!

Q What did the left **LUNG** say to the right lung?

A "We be-lung together!"

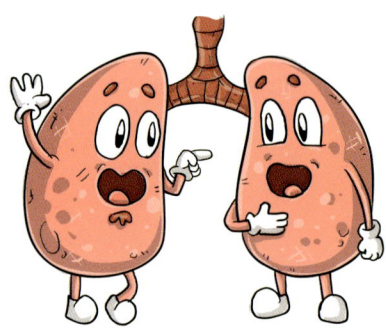

Q Why is doing **LUNGES** a great way to start your workout?

A It is a big step forward!

Q Why don't ghosts make good **MAGICIANS**?
A You can see right through their tricks!

Q What can you **MAINTAIN** without saying anything?
A Silence!

Q Why do **MANNEQUINS** lose all their friends?
A They are too clothes-minded!

Q How **MANY** monsters are good at maths?
A None, unless you Count Dracula!

Q What did everyone say to the ice-cream scoops when they got **MARRIED**?
A "Cone-gratulations!"

Q What might happen if a dentist **MARRIES** a manicurist?

A They could fight tooth and nail!

Q Why did the **MATHS** teacher insist all pupils wear glasses?

A Because she believed glasses improved division!

Q Did you hear about the cockerel that is running for **MAYOR**?

A It's a great polit-chicken!

Q How do you choose which **MECHANIC** to fix your car?

A Pick one that comes highly wreck-a-mended!

Q What's the best **MEDICINE** for cat allergies?

A An anti-hiss-tamine!

Q Did you hear about the rock band called 999 **MEGABYTES**?
A They still haven't gotten a gig!

Q Why did the chicken stop in the **MIDDLE** of the road?
A To lay it on the line!

Q What could happen if a piano fell down a **MINESHAFT**?
A You could get A-flat miner!

Q What did the cat say when it looked in the **MIRROR**?
A "Looking good, feline good!"

Q Where does a barber keep their **MONEY**?
A In a shavings account!

Q Why should you never buy flowers from a **MONK**?

A We should all try to avoid florist friars!

Q Why do **MONKEYS** carry their babies on their backs?

A Because it's too hard to drag a stroller up those trees!

Q How do **MONSTERS** like their eggs?

A Terri-fried!

Q What did the grouchy **MOON** say?

A "Just get outer my space!"

Q Why do birds sing in the **MORNING**?

A Because they don't go to school!

Q What advice did the **MOTHER** cat give her kittens?
A "With the right cat-itude, anything is paws-ible!"

Q Why did the **MOUNTAIN** love the beach?
A It wasn't shore!

Q What's a dog's favourite **MOVIE**?
A Harry Paw-ter and the Sorcerer's Bone!

Q What do you call Santa when he stops **MOVING**?
A Santa Pause!

Q What does a robot do when it gets **MUD** on its shoe?
A It reboots!

Q Is Lance an unusual **NAME** nowadays?

A "I'm not sure, but in medieval times people were called Lance a lot!"

Q Did you hear about the teenagers who only listen to **NATIONAL** anthems?

A They are real country music fans!

Q What do **NERVOUS** carpenters do?

A Bite their nails!

Q Which pet makes the loudest **NOISE**?

A A trumpet!

Q If English puns make you **NUMB**, what do maths puns make you?

A Number!

HE HE!

Q How do you cut an **OCEAN** in half?
A With a sea-saw!

Q Why did the fish get annoyed about their **OCTOPUS** friend phoning them?
A Because he tentacles late at night!

Q Did you hear about the man who called his doctor's **OFFICE** because he'd turned invisible?
A Unfortunately, nobody could see him for weeks!

Q Why is it hard to understand the word **OPAQUE**?
A The definition isn't clear at all!

Q What do you call a broken can **OPENER**?
A A can't opener!

SNICKER!

Q What did the **ORCHESTRA'S** conductor say when she found her missing music?
A "SCORE!"

Q Did you hear about the new **ORIGAMI** business?
A It folded!

Q What happens to people who don't think **ORTHOPAEDIC** shoes work?
A After they try them, they stand corrected!

Q How do rabbits travel **OVERSEAS**?
A By hare-plane!

Q What do you get if you cross an **OWL** with a skunk?
A A bird that smells, but doesn't give a hoot!

Q Why does the bald man **PACK** a comb wherever he goes?

A He just can't part with it!

Q Did you hear about the **PADDLE** at the boat store?

A It was quite an oar deal!

Q What are the similarities between a joke and a **PAPER** bag?

A Both can be recycled!

Q What's an environmentalist's favourite **PART** of a computer?

A The recycle bin!

Q Where do you take someone who is injured in a **PEEK-A-BOO** accident?

A To the ICU!

Q Who is a **PENGUIN'S** favourite relative?

A Aunt Arctica!

Q Did you hear about the new theatrical **PERFORMANCE** about puns?

A It's a play on words!

Q Why couldn't the **PHOTOGRAPHER** take pictures of the morning fog?

A He mist his chance!

Q Did you hear about the new corduroy **PILLOWCASES**?

A They're really making headlines!

Q Why was the **PILOT** fired?

A He had a bad altitude!

Q How do **PLANTS** greet each other in the morning?
A "Aloe! How's it growing?"

Q Why did the **PLUMBER** give up his job?
A He found it all too draining!

Q What do you call a **PRIEST** who becomes a lawyer?
A A father-in-law!

Q How do telephones **PROPOSE** to each other?
A They give each other a ring!

Q Why is it expensive to **PUMP** up a car's tyres at a petrol station?
A Because of inflation!

Q What do you call a **PUN** sandwich?
A A pun-ini!

Q Why is a prisoner's favourite **PUNCTUATION** mark a full stop?
A It marks the end of the sentence!

Q What's **PURPLE** and 5,000 miles long?
A The Grape Wall of China!

Q What happens if you interrupt someone working on a **PUZZLE**?
A You may hear some crosswords!

Q What did the parents say when their child asked, "Are we **PYROMANIACS**?"
A "Yes, we arson!"

Q What did one **QUARTER-POUND** burger say to the other?

A "You're bun in a million!"

Q What do you call a **QUEEN** when she climbs up a ladder?

A Your highness!

Q Why does Alice keep asking so many **QUESTIONS**?

A Because Alice is in Wonderland!

Q Did you hear about the new game called **QUIET** tennis?

A It's like regular tennis, but no one raises a racket!

Q Why do so many origami teachers **QUIT** their jobs?

A They get frustrated by all the paperwork!

Q What's the difference between a **RACE** across North America and one across Europe?

A The one across Europe eventually ends because it has a Finnish line!

Q What do you call a **RAT** that only likes to eat desserts?

A A pie-rat!

Q What does an audience shout after an avocado **RECITAL**?

A "Bravo-cado!"

Q Why can't guitars **RELAX**?

A Because they're so fretful!

Q Did you hear about the child who is designing a **REVERSIBLE** jacket?

A It will be good to see how it turns out!

Q Did you hear about the couple who met in a **REVOLVING** door?
A I think they're still going around together!

Q Do you know why I never order prawn-fried **RICE**?
A "Call me old fashioned, but I like my food to be prepared by a human!"

Q Did you know cowboys used to hang lanterns from their saddles when **RIDING** at night?
A It's the first example of saddle light navigation!

Q Do you know how to find a **RIPE** avocado?
A It's really not that hard!

Q What happened to the dog who gave birth on the side of the **ROAD**?
A She got a ticket for littering!

CACKLE!

Q What did the tomato yell to its broccoli getaway driver after **ROBBING** a bank?
A "Floret!"

Q Why was the **ROBOT** so tired after the road trip?
A It had a hard drive!

Q Did you hear that **ROCK**, paper and scissors entered a race?
A Rock has begun to roll, but paper and scissors remain stationery!

Q What do you call it when an astronaut falls asleep on a **ROCKET**?
A Spaced out!

Q What is the best country for retired **RUNNERS**?
A Iran!

Q How did the shoe **SALESPERSON** lose his job?
A His manager gave him the boot!

Q How are socks like **SCOUTS**?
A They're always pre-paired!

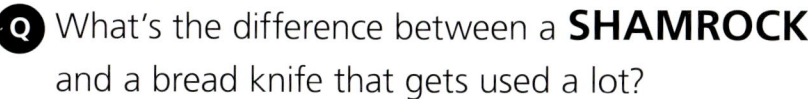

Q What's the difference between a **SHAMROCK** and a bread knife that gets used a lot?
A The shamrock is a four-leaf clover, and the knife is a four-loaf cleaver!

Q Who can **SHAVE** twenty times a day and still have a beard?
A A barber!

Q Why do all **SHEEP** look similar?
A Shear coincidence!

Q What happened to the snail that crawled out of its **SHELL**?

A It felt a little sluggish!

Q Why do burglars wear striped **SHIRTS**?

A Because they don't want to be spotted!

Q What's it like to work in a **SHOE** recycling centre?

A It can be sole destroying!

Q Why do bulls make terrible **SHOPKEEPERS**?

A They charge too much!

Q Why are all **SHOPPING** centres alike?

A Once you've seen one, you've seen a mall!

Q What happens if you get soap in your mouth while **SINGING** in the shower?
A It becomes a soap opera!

Q What's a foot long and **SLIPPERY**?
A A slipper!

Q How do **SNAILS** fight?
A They slug it out!

Q Why was the case of the stolen toilet never **SOLVED**?
A The police had nothing to go on!

Q How do trees feel in the **SPRING**?
A Re-leaved!

S

Q How does a carpenter respond when you tell them you don't want carpeted **STEPS**?

A They give you a blank stair!

Q Why isn't throwing a **SUGAR** cube at someone an act of assault?

A Because it's sugar it's not a salt!

Q How do you know the **SUN** will be back tomorrow?

A It'll dawn on you!

Q What is the **SUN'S** favourite theme park ride?

A The solar-coaster!

Q What's the best thing about **SWITZERLAND**?

A Well, the flag is a big plus!

Q Did you know that **TADPOLES** are natural storytellers?

A But when they get older, they lose their tales!

Q How do you **TALK** to a giant?

A Use big words!

Q What should you say if your **TEACHER** asks you to spell wonton backwards?

A "Not now!"

Q Where was King David's **TEMPLE** located?

A Above his ear!

Q Why was the **TONGUE-TWISTER** champion in jail for so long?

A He was given a tough sentence!

Q Have you heard the new pop song about the **TORTILLA**?
A Well, it's actually more of a wrap!

Q Which **TREES** have ghosts inside?
A Ceme-trees!

Q Why should you never **TRUST** a tree?
A They can be kind of shady!

Q Why did the **TUNA** marry the swordfish?
A Because she was such a catch!

Q What lies at the bottom of the ocean and **TWITCHES**?
A A nervous wreck!

Q What do **UNIVERSITY** professors snack on?
A Academia nuts!

Q What can go **UP** and down without moving?
A A staircase!

Q Did you hear about the woman who fell onto an **UPHOLSTERY** machine?
A She's fully recovered!

Q What do you call the hair above a mouse's **UPPER** lip?
A A mouse-tache!

Q What do you throw away when you want to **USE** it?
A An anchor!

Q What should you do on **VACATION** in Italy's capital?
A Rome around and pasta time!

Q Why did the cleaner decide to sell a **VACUUM** cleaner?
A It was just collecting dust!

Q What did the dog say to its **VALENTINE**?
A "I'm mutts about you!"

Q Why are **VAMPIRES** always so tired?
A They work the graveyard shift!

Q Which **VEGETABLE** can your father make with scissors?
A Pa snips!

Q What type of TV shows do **VETS** like to watch?
A Duck-umentaries!

Q Why did the **VIKING** buy a second-hand boat?
A He couldn't a-fjord a new one!

Q What do you call **VIKINGS** who don't eat animal products?
A Nor-vegans!

Q What's small and red and has a rough **VOICE**?
A A hoarse radish!

Q Where do polar bears **VOTE**?
A The North Poll!

Q Did you hear about the angry **WAFFLE** iron?
A He just flipped!

Q Why are **WAITERS** the most impressive people in a restaurant?
A They bring so much to the table!

Q What do you call a **WALKING** stick that makes someone walk faster?
A A hurricane!

Q What does C.S. Lewis keep at the back of his **WARDROBE**?
A Narnia business!

Q What is a car's **WEAKEST** point?
A The nut holding the steering wheel!

Q What has fangs and **WEBBED** feet?
A Count Duckula!

Q Did you hear about the couple who met on a dating **WEBSITE**?
A They just clicked!

Q How do you know if you are at an emotional **WEDDING**?
A Check if the cake is in tiers!

Q What are the strongest days of the **WEEK**?
A Saturday and Sunday, the rest are weak days!

Q What kind of **WHALE** is the saddest?
A A blue whale!

Q Why do teachers love **WHITEBOARDS**?
A They're re-markable!

Q What do you call the **WIFE** of a hippie?
A A Mississippi!

Q Why shouldn't you visit an expensive **WIG** shop?
A It's too high a price toupee!

Q Why did the builder hate glass **WINDOWS**?
A Because they are such a pane!

Q Why did **WOOLLY** mammoths become extinct?
A They became irr-elephant!

Q Why can't you lie to **X-RAY** technicians?
A They can see right through you!

Q Why is school life like a **YO-YO**?
A It has its ups and downs!

Q Why did the **YOUNG** horse practise galloping in private?
A He didn't want to make a foal of himself!

Q What should you say to the person who invented **ZERO**?
A "Thanks for nothing!"

Q Did you hear about the **ZOO** featuring only flightless birds?
A Unfortunately, it never really took off!

CACKLE!

SNICKER!

GUFFAW!

HE HE!

HAH!

Published by:
Green Android Ltd
49 Beaumont Court
Upper Clapton Road
London
E5 8BG
United Kingdom

Illustrated by Vasco Icuza
Text compiled by Toby Reynolds
Edited by Shaheen Bilgrami

ISBN 978-1-912188-32-1
Copyright © Green Android Ltd 2023

All rights reserved. No part of this publication may be reproduced, stored in a retrieval system, or transmitted in any form or by any means, electronic, mechanical, photocopying, recording or otherwise without the prior written permission of the copyright owner.

Printed and bound in Malaysia, June 2023